Shadow Tongue

poems by

Kim Cope Tait

Finishing Line Press
Georgetown, Kentucky

Shadow Tongue

ACKNOWLEDGMENTS

Grateful acknowledgment is made to the editors of the following periodicals in which these
poems first appeared:

Bamboo Ridge: "Wild Thing"
Dewpoint Literary Journal: "Dreaming of Dahlias"
Hamakua Times: "Waipiʻo Redemption"
Hawaii Pacific Review: "Love Song to Waipiʻo"
Hunger Mountain: "Three Fish"
Iota: "To Grandma Neva"
Magma: "Adrian II"
Merge Poetry: "Skinny Dip"
Poetry Canada: "Heritage"
Poetry Miscellany: The seven poems of the "Rosie Sonnets"
Poetry Quarterly: "El Retiro"
Tipton Poetry Journal: "In Vain"

And deep gratitude to Jordan Jones of Leaping Dog Press for first publishing my chapbook
called *Element*, where "Whisper," "Sun Sestina," and "Me & Mrs. Dalloway" first appeared.

Richard Jackson, Ralph Angel, Mary Ruefle, Pat Schneider, Kevin Clark, and Valerie
Martinez: you each have had (and continue to have) a pivotal role in shaping the way I
move in the world of words. How do I begin to thank you?

Joan Logghe, what a happy surprise to meet you and become your friend. Thank you
for your encouragement and for loving me up, along with my work. It has made all the
difference.

Publisher: Leah Maines
Editor: Christen Kincaid
Cover Art: Maureen O'Neill
Author Photo: Dwaine Tait
Cover Design: Elizabeth Maines McCleavy

Printed in the USA on acid-free paper.
Order online: www.finishinglinepress.com
                  also available on amazon.com

Author inquiries and mail orders:
Finishing Line Press
P. O. Box 1626
Georgetown, Kentucky 40324
U. S. A.

Table of Contents

Prologue

...in the cave of my idolatry

Sin of Resistance

Truth of Words

Sin of Dreaming

Yes, I say, Yes

Self Embrace

Mango lisp. Wild, open mouth of my dreaming.
Shadow tongue in the cave of my idolatry.

I forgive you for living at the edge of your want.

Open funnel of my lotus love. Pale ash from the
quiet explosion of the mind clings to my moist skin.

I forgive you for dying.

I forgive myself for the sin of resistance, of judging
my impulses. Sin of dreaming it into life and

gliding away from it. Oh.

Soft hum of forgiveness winds its way up my spine,
lifts itself up through the elements, growing lighter:

earth, water, fire, air, ether, light. Consciousness.

Secrets peel themselves from my hair and I am naked
in the truth of my words. Swivel self, know and be,

Yes, I say, *yes.*

...in the cave of my idolatry

The Adrian Sonnets

I.

When Adrian died in the quarry, it was like the sky opening up, dropping the dark
over his mother, stars sticking like feathers. Unable to move, she let her womb
be emptied, let joy be redistributed as it must. The end of this lanky, stark-
grinned boy meant her family broken into islands, glossy white ocean foam

rushing between. She built a shrine to him in her bedroom, as her husband
pretended to watch football on TV. Athletic awards, senior portraits, child
poems. She would lie for hours next to that monument and with one hand
trace the stream of prayers disappearing between her lips and the ceiling. Wild

for her son, she howled her grief from the open bathroom window, sat
on the toilet tank and cupped her small breasts in her hands, nursing spirits
as she rocked forward and back, yellow square of light gently framing that
figure for the neighbors. Finally she turned her back to the pale darkness, its

breath passing over her like promise. No one spoke of her absence in town
or in the church; hers was the way of quiet sanction, the absence of sound.

II.

The quiet sanction of liquid breathed into lungs, of life submerged in water dark
as root beer, pooled in the pit of Rita's stomach as she watched her mother sleep,
lips moving slightly—the constant prayer of the retroactively vigilant. To mark
the fifth day, she climbed the oak in the yard, her tree-frog legs carrying her deep

into the branches of memory. She stayed for hours, holding her
brother's Yosemite Sam t-shirt to her face, breathing his scent, rocking the way
she'd seen her mother do. Later, Jessie's voice drifted up to her like a zephyr,
and finally she answered to the girl who'd loved him, she knew. That day,

Jessie wore her pain like stones in her throat, and they sat cross-legged on Rita's bed
until midnight, swapping stories about Adrian and his skateboard, Adrian and
his dog Seth, Adrian with the earth under his feet. Rita shook curls of fire red
hair from her eyes like shaking dreams from sleep. With one pale hand
on her heart, she laughed his laugh and glanced *his* grin at Jessie who

leaned forward then and softly kissed her on her pink lips—to Adrian always true.

III.

Strange the way Jessie reacted when Norma told her the news,
Adrian sinking to the bottom instead of floating to the top: she
ran onto the slanting lawn in front of Mo's, said she had to choose
a star to carry in her throat, let one sandal dangle crazily

from her ankle, brown leather strap binding broken shoe to body.
Her wild prayers spilled into the air and tangled themselves in
the whine of freeway traffic: a long and braided treaty
with the god of her dreams. She spun around then, her thin

neck stretching with the points of the swallowed star. She pressed
strange fists into her stomach, into her breasts, looked to Norma
crying in the doorway of Mo's but could only see the light that dressed
Norma's body there. *Save me.* She sent the words to form a

ring around the hole where her star had been, but they fell on
the grass beside her. The bouyancy in the air was gone.

IV.

The bouyancy in the air was gone, the sky flat, Adrian already dead
when Jessie arrived. Rita gently wiped gel from his temples, the world
already cocked on her left shoulder, skewing her posture. Adrian's head
looked strangely mounted on his pale and bloated neck, but his fingers curled

naturally like sleep. Jessie whispered his poem back to him, her lips
touching his ear. *I know and you know, I can see through the window.*
She had wanted a love poem. *Jump the magic, it's up to you.* Hand on hip,
she'd complained: I don't even understand it. *Hurry up, the sky is blue.* Now,

his words mingled with whispers from the white hall: the chaplain,
and his parents. *I went this way, you said before. It is you*
whom I adore. And his grandmother, quiet and still, in the corner of the room, again

considering the inversion of life. Present at the death of a grandchild. Through

taut air, Jessie lifted his head, cradled it with one arm—*I see deep into your eyes*—
her breast spilling into the space between jaw and shoulder—*...no time to criticize.*

V.

Spilling into a space not meant for her, Jessie mourned him for many
years. We in town tried not to hear when she told us about Adrian's ghost
coming to her in her sleep: on the hill behind the granary, in the chapel, mahogany
pews under tremulous fingers, her head tilted to one side. Her Heavenly Host

looked on from the banister, Baby Jesus with a man's face. Adrian's breath
on her shoulder as she let the Virgin Mary drink her with her eyes. Orange
candles reflected on brown skin. She mouthed his eulogy again. His death
twisted him around her heart, made him the thing she could love as strange.

She seemed to sink to the bottom of the quarry, and to rise
like a displaced trout, all iridescent in the sun, her fishlips mouthing his
praise. When a boy drowns before a girl may construct words from his sighs,
she may disappear into their almost love. Jessie lay on this

bank, heaving dry oxygen into her fish body, dangling her fin as if to give
a handhold to poor Orpheus, her mind straining purity like a sieve.

VI.

Jesse's need to be worthy of an angel's love
made you want to hold her head in your hands,
push her hair back and back, soft whisper of
a curl in the fine, kelp-colored strands,

your own want sifting through it like light.
Impossibility made her beautiful, radiant. Yet
she wanted what would not save her, would fight
the instinct to heal. Reckless for grace, she knelt
before Christ, bloody palms opened to her

like a question. Sinless, nearly nameless
now, she was clairvoyant, deep in prayer:
she saw her wet mouth slipping across

Father Crane's cheek as he refused her, for surely
he would, his own desire crippled by his goodness.

Praying to a Broken Boy

This is the wafer I hold on my tongue
pretending to be Catholic.
The priest with marshmallow skin
tells me I will always be a stepchild
in the congregation, but I am willing
to be saved second-hand. I'm not picky.

I am the girlfriend of a dead boy
who wishes she'd given herself to him
before that day, wishes she'd tasted him,
even once, before he spilled away from her
and into the next life.

Broken boy with crushed glass still in his hair.
I mopped spackled blood from his bloated skin
and whispered prayers into his ear. *I love you,*
Goodbye Adrian, Goodbye Adrian, Goodbye
Adrian, and there's not much time between
yes and no on a black hole monitor,
your heart measured in the peaks and valleys
of a green line.

No, you were not faithful. Not in those last weeks.
How to be faithful to a girl who wants to be perfect,
whose icy morality had separated her from her own kind
and provided little comfort in the hours of despair.
No, you deserved a little pleasure, a little sin, flavor. Oh.
Forgive me for wanting so to be good
that I could not see myself. I let you go to her.

It was *my* name you called out in the emergency room.
My name you pushed through tears and the mythical
strength of the shocked and dying. How I fear it was your
guilt that propelled the cry, your fear that I did not know
that I occupied the center of your heart, for this fear was mirrored
in my own: fear that you did not hear my love as I poured it
into your ears, your grandmother rocking gently, only feet away.

White circles like petals on your forehead, each attached
to a blue wire leading to the beyond. Why did you follow them?
Why did you climb them like vines—into death? I would have
lifted each of your organs to my pink lips, kissed them alive
and carried you into a shared future. That's what I promised
your body, even as your spirit was peeling itself away,
shuddering in the wake of my love, and leaving the way it came.

Becoming Maridel

I slip into your thin, pale skin, too weak
for hot baths or the friction that comes
with loss. Spidery veins reveal me, speak
the desire that breaks me. At the tomb
of my memory, I offer self and solace.

I become the mother I saw in a snapshot:
a boy captured in sunlight, mid-air in his
wild leap from lawn to glinting water.
I am she, who stands at the edge of the pool,
colorful beach towel in hand, expectant.
My boy will not come to me now.

From inside this skin, Maridel, yours…
I am not more than I was before, but changed:
swelling with the grief that becomes my love
and is turned back again and again
to what aches, what saves. I am the mother
of these two. Your hurt teaches me to love them
in a way I could not have dreamed up had I not
seen you, known you, become you, even
for a moment.

Sin of Resistance

Dreaming of Dahlias

The reality of it drips down
around the window frame,
as from the curtain rod, or
perhaps it has seeped in
between the glass and casing,
to show us, metaphorically
of course, who we really are.
How a second earlier, or
a second later—the wave
of a hand—or its absence—
could have changed the course,
incrementally, but just so,
to accelerate movement
toward an utterly different
destination. Today, dahlias
spike the air with their beauty
and we think, as our feet
crunch across gravel bordered
by hedges clipped in the shape
of a green labyrinth, that beauty
is all there is. Beyond beauty:
the nothing. If a radiant
half-moon, tipped on its side
can generate tears, then it seems
the source of grief or joy
must be the same—ever.
Our relentless desire
to experience beauty
might even be at the heart
of gravitational theory.
The Bahais say it is love
that holds the atoms together,
keeps the electrons circling the
nucleus in their ceaseless orbit.
But what of love? Isn't love
just what happens when
we become beauty?

To Grandma Neva

Your hands are knotted and bent, skin like dappled
litmus stretched across the arches of knuckles rising
like the Sierra Nevadas from pinkie to pointer.

You turn your wrist to reveal the Rook card in your hand,
raise your eyebrows like two parentheses capsized, Smile.
I know you came to my son last night. In his dream.

I wanted to know what you said to him. To receive a
message from the other side. I asked him again and again
until finally his four-year old heart shaped the answer

that suited him. *She said, "Heaven is great,"* he told me
with a perfectly straight face. *And her eyes were very big.*
How long is a life, I want to ask him. Though this is the very

question he posed to me just last week. *When I stop breathing
will I die*, he wanted to know. I lied and said he would never die,
would never stop breathing and wrapped my arms so tightly around him

I was able to embrace myself. So you visited. And you didn't speak.
My son has always loved you best. You. Best. You moved toward him,
touched his face with the backs of those spidery fingers and left. Me.

Perfect

The gossamer wish for permanence makes its cold promise
as quickly as the lips can shape the word *please*. I blow
at what candles might flicker in the dark underside of this
holiness, but it is my love that collapses again, though

it pulls the fear inside of itself, roots itself in the heart
or the stomach. Destroyed by my desire to keep
and keep you, I am swallowed by the sin of art-
less hope. With the same fury, I am reconstructed, sweet

religion for the faithless. Lifted up out of the ash,
ancient ruin of what we give. Dust. Spinning out
into the universe, this: my love for you, my son. Fresh,
perfect torque on the silence of knowing. Night sky of

the starless sleeping self exploded out into the world,
the excellent and raw wound of motherhood.

Sun Sestina

I close my hand over the boy's
hand. He can see that my sun
has set into my throat, knows
my wanting, feels it like an animal
in the dark underbelly of these days.
We breathe unwords, move across

water on our bellies, on our feet. Across
this distance I sing down the boy:
sing the belligerent truth of my silence. Day
of undoing, come. My language is a big sun,
yellow and bald in its laughter, the animal
radiance of this heat.   In this moment I know

there is no place for this thing. I know
the impossibility, the imperfection that spans across
every single star, white pointy eyes of animals
that haunt the dream, lick their lips, sigh the boy,
sigh the name, hunt the motionless sun,
mother of them all. They will not find her today,

caught in my throat as she is. I swallow and day
becomes mine. Owner of illusion, ready to know
what can't be known. Poised on this brink: sun
burning a hole in my gut, burning, burning across
generations of lovers in their galaxies, orbit of this boy,
this light. I turn in the dark exterior, my animal

want rolling inside my rib cage like marbles, animal
hunger, animal need, infant truth burgeoning. Day
dawns in my pelvis, lifting itself down, and the boy
turns away, walks. How can he know
the meaning of a sun rising from my navel, moving across
the planet of my body, glistening the undoing of all the suns

ever arched in desire across this fatal sky. O sun
of being, sun of mine, lift me into that orbit. Animals,

move in my heart, make me weak, breathe across
the taut strings of my self, create a music so fair that days
will move inside of it. I move in this unknown
rhythm. Become soil. Root. Leaf of what the boy

raises like a banner above his head, across sunlight
so fervent in its heat, boy in the animal dream, the
day peaking in his man-heart. Know this: love.

Waiting for Practice to End

from the memoirs of a soccer mom

Treetops
pierce
the canopy
of sky
without
deflating it
somehow.
I expect it
to pop and
shudder and
spill itself
over the foliage,
but it remains
buouyant, alive
with the Swiss
mountain air,
and a blue so
vibrant it sings
wordlessly,
without sound:
vibration of color,
of oxygen
imbued with
something that is
just about to happen,
hanging there,
like this. *Like this.*

Wild Thing

I wrap myself tightly in these days, swallow what
I can and hold the rest under my tongue. Greedy for
you, my son, I am paralyzed by a fear so great
I can only recognize it as my love. Manic and more

than weary, I want what is already mine. Want it
and want it again. "We'll eat you up, we love
you so," cry the beasts, the wild things, and not
in voices frightening or frightened. High above

the cover of their jungle, I hover, their voices ringing
in my head like a bell, tolling the impossibility of
a mother's love. I become what I envision, singing
the truth of life unfolding in one's hand, the beauty, the

weight of it. I hold you in the palm of my heart, kiss you
fiercely, wild thing that I am, voracious and broken in my love.

Me and Mrs. Dalloway

What I am, I say equivocally and step into the waves.
It is a whisper, and like everything else, it only
has meaning for me. There is still comfort in this.
And terror. Memory flickers across a pale horizon:
touching my sons. Their apples for cheeks in my
hands. Their clipped hair as my fingers move
against its angle, gently now. Mommy.

I feel so strange. Foreigner in my own edemic body.
I float. Far out at sea. Me and Clarissa. Bobbing
at the surface. *To live even one day is so dangerous,*
she reminds me, and I recognize it as the song that
lives me; it fills the air above our heads. Dangerous.
Dangerous. It is a resounding threat. Echo of a
promise. A yes. This undoing. Me. We come undone.
We two out on the sea, we unravel, disclose what we are
to a hostile jury of gulls, poised mid-flight and hovering
over what they do not know and cannot guess.

I am a shambles, I observe, but this is nothing new.
I take Clarissa in my thin arms, but she kisses me
on my pink lips and begins to sink. I let her
fawn-colored hair slip softly through my fingers
as she descends in shafts of indecisive light. She
leaves me: modern-day Ophelia. She. Good bye,
Clarissa. What can I be but this thing that remains?
What can I be but this?

Truth of Words

One Year After the Telegram

Her heart has slipped down her left leg, a free
agent now, settled in her heel. Beating
still. Moving the blood. Stirring it. And she
will sleep with Dallas tonight. Something

about him that's not so hard. She sees her
self floating in his irises, sees her
self shudder under his climax. Sees her
body flatten under his weight and then

lift itself on the wave of unmemory,
un-consciousness, wave of a sigh. Moments
gone, just like that. Nothing in their place. She
opens her hibiscus lips and says, "O," has rent

the letters into pieces, reassigned them.
Moribund Insomniac Azaleas.

Pantoum for Grandpa Gordy

Cull the clotted clouds out of
a pale blue sky, and there we find
the history of disappearance.
How a Sabre jet can be and not be

in a pale blue sky, and there we find
the story of you, how you are the ellipsis,
how a Sabre jet can be and not be
the way we see ourselves, metal glinting

the story of you, how you are the ellipsis
in the collective memory of a family,
the way we see ourselves, metal glinting
at the edge of cold earth—snow.

In the collective memory of a family,
I stole you. How I imagined you
at the edge of cold earth—snow
in your hair, your love rising in flames.

I stole you. How I imagined you,
the history of disappearance
in your hair, your love rising in flames,
culling out the clotted clouds.

Grandpa Joe's Birthday

Two years after her son is among ghosts
crouching in the trees of North Korea
she puts on her violet dress without pantyhose,
grips the porcelain floor of a claw-foot tub

with brown toes. Nails clipped to the skin.
I change it now. As much air as words. She wears
her bitterness on her mouth, matte red, thin-
lipped sneer as she takes her long black hair

into her hands, readies the blade of a
kitchen knife, runs it across flesh, pale
underbelly of faith gone awry. Red
and wet, her want begins to spill, soak

chiffon sleeves fluttering. MIA means wait
and please, but her son is a shade among trees.

The Rosie Sonnets

I.

I'll be home before Christmas this year. It is a promise at the end
of a letter about MIGS and F-86 missions and *Rosie I miss
you, I miss the boys, I saw a fire-orange star bend
the blue of the sky and turn to ash, yesterday. Rosie this*

is something I must tell you, and then the silence that followed, worse
than the tremulous sound of waiting. In the night she listened
for the cricket's voice, but heard only the hollow music of herself. Hers
was a song of fluid want, like gasoline on water, swirling away the end

of an hour that was four years. The black coral hair he loved became
red then platinum, blond then auburn, until it was dull brown wisps
tucked under various wigs, and the wanting became bitter, his name
like a mackeral under her tongue. Grief cupped in her hand, the lisp

of her life could barely be heard in the voices of her sons, even then
beginning to fade, even then dissolving into memories of men.

II.

Dissolved in the memories of men. This dim image of a woman.
She marries a schoolteacher. That tall drink of water with eyes
like Kansas who calls her Rosie, paints a red bud on his F-86 when
he goes to Korea. Stays up nights under bursting shrapnel skies,

writes letters to her, to the boys. She wears the red apron of these
days and pins her raven hair at the sides, black wings measuring this
distance in secret. Johnny resembles him the most. His laugh a breeze
that moves the grass. He'll become a pilot. Remember his

father with his body, with his life. Danny is too young. Memory still
in its infancy, these moments sift through it like salt. He will remember
instinctively, fingertips brushing a face, a name. But the youngest will
carry his own brand of bitterness, wear it as a coat, and return to her

in middle age, himself become the mother he saw slowly slip into
the music of a Patti Page song, into the swinging cage of a cockatoo.

III.

She sings Patti Page, Doris Day, a voice like velvet
drawn across pale shoulders, sings while she works, sings
under arched eyebrows, a mole like Marilyn Monroe. We let
our father listen to her memory as he speaks, rings

of light spilling out from his lips, a disturbance in the water. She,
whose face is furrowed with worry and years of cigarette smoke, face
powder soft and pink over open pores-*she was beautiful,* he
says—and the dog in his lap reclines across his thigh. We try to trace

our lines of history through him, but he left home at fifteen
when Bob shot his .22 through her window. The neat hole
was something through which an irretrievable life had passed. Seen
through the eyes of a boy who saved himself because the whole

couldn't, these days are cold and white at the edges, like a dream
sequence in a soap opera, and perhaps her caged lovebirds are to blame.

IV.

Perhaps her caged lovebirds are to blame for what followed the war.
The trucker was first: Dallas. *Or was it Clay?* There were trailers,
chickens, gardens and dust, a third marriage to a loving drunk. More
children than seeds. And why *not* blame the birds?

It was Bob who died in her arms, so she started sleeping under newspaper
on the couch. It was Aunt Emily who came and finally said *no more:*
when she found Christine, five years old, in a dress and no panties, her
belly bloated empty, hot iron in hand, pile of clothes on the floor.

It was my father they finally called when it seemed she was too wild
to be what she was. When her words stopped making sense, when she didn't

get up, even to bathe. Years old, he left a new wife and seedling child
in their small country home, drove to the house he left. In the end, spent,

he called the police to take her away. *You are not my son,* she cried,
I never knew you, as they touched her wild hair and helped her inside.

V.

I never knew you, she said, and perhaps it was the truth. My dad was steady,
didn't cry. I imagine him quiet that day, sullen, as they closed
the door after her, trailing her pink terrycloth robe. You're never ready
to rethink the ridiculous. As they drove away, he stood in the road,

documents crumpled in his hand, white dog sniffing at his shoes. He
had not been back to the old house, and he looked to it now, thrown
against sky and still leaning uncomfortably, sighing his scattered family.
His daughter had her eyes, and a tuft of her black hair, a crown

of memory. He had always known that the past was inescapable,
and yet he ran, pausing only to breathe an ellipsis into recollection. They
would have no words for that moment. She would return, too, unable
to remember or speak what had been. She would place a glass ashtray

on the arm of the sofa, a sweating glass of iced tea on a metal coaster,
and fade into the yellowed walls of that house as it gently forgave her.

VI.

She faded into old age and into the yellowed walls
of her house, covered them with contact paper, hung
scissors, magazine cut-outs, keychains, paper dolls
from red and yellow thumbtacks. Her life, strung

across this background, layers of smokey residue, her heart
fell silent: in time it is only a matter of time
before MIA becomes less than a promise, and the art
of mourning swallowed her in its beauty. In time

her knotted jaws were set against news, against hope. Numb,
she let it all go. The three men after. Her children. The four
who left. And at what point had she succumbed
to the blue light of the TV? A woman's life is lost well before

her death. Wed now to the ivy that creeps across her siding,
pale green, in her slippered feet she talks and laughs of nothing.

VII.

In her slippered feet she talks and laughs of nothing. Her long, gray
hair is pulled into a ponytail, tied with blue yarn. Housedress
lies on her shoulders like litmus, in the heat of the afternoon. Today
she accepts us as her visitors: we file into the living room and press

ourselves into the pall of that space. For twenty
minutes we make small talk on her green couch in a row,
dangling pink balls from an afghan throw tapping lightly
against our calves. She says again she doesn't know

what happened to the box of photos she had when she lived
in the trailor out on Carpenter. She says it to the girl
with eyes she knows, the girl who leans forward to ask. She will give
nothing of him to us: where we begin is an end for her. A curl

crosses her lips. She surveys me and closes her mouth
gently over the secrets that should have redeemed us both.

Bird House

A bird lies in the crabgrass in the yard. It's so small
it could fit in the hollow of your throat, but you can
see that it's a jay. It has fallen twice: once from the tall
birch, softly wooded nest awkward, spreading like a fan

amid anemic branches. Once from the sky-colored
birdhouse where Mary Anne set it, meaning to save
it from the neighbor's cats. Tiny bird balcony, cold
bed for a fledgling. Safe, she thought, and she gave

it a push away from the edge. Still, limp and wet
with birth, it pushed with small and crippled wings, not to fly
but to move heavily away from the birdhouse, from what
held it, might rescue it, and dropped like a too-honest reply.

It landed soundlessly, Rosie curiously noting the special
stillness of fear, her cigarette smoking itself in its tray.

Heritage

Some notion of our story is sung in the nod of her head,
soft pillow of opened palm, slow gesture of hand through
still air. I offer my son as proof of self, proof of said
connection and memory, though he is fair and soft, eyes too

blue green, their ocean not yet swallowed by doubt—whatever
it is that changes us. She's wearing an orange clip of yarn around
her thin, gray ponytail. It's almost as if with it I could tie up her
loveless drawl, the gentle distance between lips and the sound

uttered in the moments before death, soft exhalation of yes
and please. Almost worth looking for the skein. A tiny windmill
sits motionless on the porch. Made of waxed milk cartons, this
artifact is evidence of some creative streak. Or of the malignant

desire to flaunt the kind of boredom that chews at the heart, strange
common trait, the way I have taken up crocheting, though it stultifies.

Red

I let my hair, fine and long, fall like a shroud
over a pale white image of myself because where
does the seed of self begin, if not in dying? Proud
of who knows what, I rest my brown hand there,

touch the bluest eye of my grandfather. And who
remembers this life? Who can remember who we are
if my grandmother pulls the photos of our people through
the eye of a needle, and leaves them to smolder in the far

reaches of her mind's eye. What am I if she lays the dead
body of her husband over the trail of our roaming and turns
away? Sky falls to earth and this is what I see: red.
Red earth, red skin, a handful of feathers, and four red urns

full of the ashes of my Irish fathers. I begin here on this thin
moment between earth and sky. I lift the death shroud and *begin*.

The Long Goodbye

You have become a myth for me.
Some hint of self, enigmatic reflection
of my history. You take with you
all the secrets we wanted to hear you
speak, all of the reasons we imagined up—
or never could. How do I say goodbye to you?

Something about you that was lovely,
beautiful. Blazing comet moving
in your irregular orbit, leaving sparks, light
in your wake, but never pausing to look back
and see what you had sown.

If the night sky was your arena,
you are still moving there now,
your broken heart finally shed and left
on some suburban lawn where it fell
as your soul lifted on air and became light,
weightless for the first time in so many years.

O, we languish in the light that trails behind you,
lift our faces and make our goodbye
the kind of greeting we wanted you to have.
Welcome to the sky, welcome to freedom,
welcome to the liberation of existing
in memory alone. Glide into what you always
wanted to be. I don't presume. I know.
Because it's what we all want.
Anonymity somehow. The kind of freedom
that means not shrinking from the truth.

Blessings upon you, Rosie. You were brave
and this life was again and again unkind,
each year a moment in a very long goodbye.

The Sin of Dreaming

The Study of Perceiving

Waipi'o Redemption

See the pale atoms lift and glide on air,
pastel marriage of water and sunlight—
perfect motion of what we find there.

We quietly savor this thing we share
as the waterfall sings our names in flight,
and each pale atom lifts and glides on air.

Minutes explode and move beyond the hour—
Burdens tumble up, float to that great height.
Perfect motion of what we find there.

Water surges from the jagged pali where
Pele's outline reclines against receding night—
see the pale atoms lift and glide on air

and sing the truth of the love we bear,
our bodies moving through refracted light:
perfect motion of what we find there.

We rake our hands through the sea and dare
To lift ourselves into this moving might.
See the pale atoms lift and glide on air,
perfect motion of what we find there.

Skinny Dip

for Meghann

Our pale bodies glisten in the stark light
of a salad bowl moon. Shivering bulbs line
the water: beacons in a motionless night
send green flames across the fine

and glinting surface of sea. White skin in
the shape of a bikini, punctuated
vaguely by faint nipples, nebulous, thin
lines of our dim features striated

by moving shadow—*this is what it is
to be young*, I think, and plunge off the end
of the launch ramp, laughing. Beyond us,
beyond the break wall, small waves lift and

crumble, whispering the passage of time
to us as we lift ourselves like tightrope
walkers on air, spinning, tossing the lime-
colored sigh of our looping spiral: hope

and longing and this transient satisfaction.
Full-throated cry of a moment's seizure.
Rebellion of somebody's English teacher
naked on the Kawaihae jetty—our sheer

liberation. *Ha ha ha*, we think of
saying as we swim and glide in water,
stand atop a tower like nymphs, like love,
like schoolgirls aching with want. We leap

into darkness, flipping, landing, splashing.
Yes, we nod, *yes*, and later as we sleep
Queen Mab flutters across our eyelids, fishing
for dreams, and a slow trickle of saltwater
finds its way out of our ears.

In Vain

Last night Ben Harper, bathed in indigo,
gave himself to a sold-out crowd in Geneva.

Six encore ballads, and still, he couldn't find
his way. The music was perfect—simple gift of

self—but his consternation— as he looked out
into the darkness, this is what he saw: misdirected

enthusiasm, passion for sound and not meaning.
Love of the body and not what breathes it.

We saw it—in the triangle between
someone's jaw and their shoulder, in the flickering

image between arms raised in adulation, we saw him
stand still—how a dream of compassion

can disappear into a smoke ring. Being rooted to
the floor by the closeness of bodies all pressing in

made us sleepy. And profoundly sad.
The incongruity of our reception with what you gave…

it was like the spotlights moving over the bodies
in the mezzanine, how they moved quickly,

indiscriminately, too fast for anything to come into focus.
Though there was light, we still couldn't see their faces.

And neither could you when you gazed up from your microphone.
When you stood at the edge of the stage and launched

your blessing into the smoke-filled air, unamplified,
we thought we could see you for real. We stood very still

and took you in, though it hurt. When you stepped back

and waited for the cheering to end so you could say

God's name, that was when we knew. You.
You who had discovered our limits.

Three Fish

Three fish and I might be dreaming. I fear
I might be god, and this is what I hold in my hands
like a wet mackeral: the possibility of knowing nothing
more divine than the pathetic, fish-like thing that I am.

I gasp for breath, fish gills still lurching open and
closed. No way to absorb the oxygen of dry air, O—
the certainty of this fear, its pale fins glistening in muted
sunlight. The alive portal into what might be if we

let it, what might disintegrate and build itself again
in our midst. Holy trinity of fish: bread of my body,
wine of my spirit, pink lotus of my consciousness.
Three fish, three fears, three visions of self panting

behind the door. Yes and please and why must it
always reach this pitch? What is the need, what
is the weight of this thing in my hands—green,
slippery fish body of what I refuse to name—O!

I turn and the fish grow large behind me. They
swell and expand and I feel their slick bodies against
my bare back. This, I think, this is how it goes. This
is how it grows, this is the way I give myself to fear.

Love Song to Waipi'o

The visceral language of the Valley shivers us awake.
Here, even the way the sky opens up is a triangle.
The bodies of the white birds, the ordered pattern of their flight,
the tops of pine trees, the path the rain takes from earth to sea: all
open into three angles that sing the geometric precision
of this place. This water holds the nascent memory of form,

though it shifts and undulates beneath us. In our minds, form
undoes itself again, as we toss ourselves up and wake
to a new distance, an unmemory, the voiceless and precise
whisper of a goddess whose name is on our tongues—three angled
figure swinging from a mirror—how to speak it? –precious all
that remains of what felt at one time like love, like flight.

How we spill ourselves into this landscape. Hoping, we fly
to its rugged sanctuary and listen as it forms
the words we could never speak. The soft exhalation of all
who careen into this space: we. Uncertain of our place but awake
to its beauty and tumbling ourselves into the triangle
of the river mouth waiting, waiting. Oh, this is precisely

how we seek redemption—plunge our bodies into precision:
salt water edged with morning light. Baptism of imperfect flight,
and O, the inadequacy of the word. Guilty trinity
of the self: spirit and mind resist body, captain of forms,
body imperfect and full with desire. Mind refuses to wake
to the whole, embrace what is good if not divine. But all

of the old impossibilities disappear here and we
let the animal dream whisper itself to sleep, precise
outline of a need that no longer haunts, no longer wakes
us in the night or in our sleepwalk days. This is the flight
of transformation, what the Valley gives to us, the wild form
of our willingness to touch even these white, triangular

birds laboring across a slice of peerless sky. Triangles
emerge in our vision, and there is a kind of balance in all

of it: the way our memories of one another take the form
the river gives them. The way we can accept the precise
answer the black sand makes to our questioning: shhh. The flight
of our senses as they receive the wordless sigh and wake.

The goddess shimmers and turns on air, her triangular form
all golden in the sun: it creeps over the mountains as we wake
to the arc of love's flight and the precision of trusting what is light.

Whisper

Voice passes between
lips is breath is
a prism. It is my
penance my
lament, the ways in which
I know myself as other
than what I want to be.
I am
vulgar, crude, untamed, mis-
shapen. I am the blue
of that background, dappled
with the shadows of unself of
wanting and wanting and
finally—Nothing. The emptiness
of a vast field. My hair as
long and bending shafts of
wheat and grass and
dandelions gone to
seed. I am the un-
mother the un-woman. Super,
Hyper, over, thing of
my blindness. I grope in
darkness the cold air of the un-
day. Un-love. Un-language.
Dis-being.

We Evolve

We two, we struggle underwater, tangled in our own hair
like kelp. Brown bulbs lift themselves toward surface but

we are enmeshed in the fleshy limbs of this gelatinous net,
what we promised each other as children, as betrothed, our

faces fresh and beaming—what we believed it all meant,
what we understand now…or at least descry in the nebulous

periphery of our experience. How you still cling to me, grasp
at wrists, ankles as they free themselves and are caught up again

in the old belief—old vision of how a woman should move.
You grasp, hold me long, though I've already flown, already

disappeared into my own thoughts—irrecoverable distance of
consciousness—writhing physicality the ghost of self. Shell

echoes with murmurs of a past that imbues the water with
its light like flakes of gold or the glowing atoms of this kind

of love. I love you still, though my heart has sprung its long
tether, reeled out into the orbit of my desire: as anemic as it

had become, it sets me on fire now. I ignite, my soul ablaze,
my hair in flames. I am set afire, says the angel. I am set afire.

Yes, I Say, Yes

Conversation With a Crow

I.

Clock cracks each second behind my head—
I never heard it once while we spoke—murmur
of the fantastic, the divine. Honest connection
of cells, of blood, of feathers and faith.

II.

How it moves, how it goes, how it slows
honeyed breath in ears like flowers, scent
of this shared longing. Tilt the head like
this, speak the words burgeoning freshwater
springs and fire in the mind, the heart, the holy
palms sealed and stowed like this, like this. Oh.

III.

Language fills my consciousness, soothes like music,
like the sky around a full moon, river that seems
not to move at all but to provide a glossy mirror
to the trees along its steep banks: their images mottle
the surface, give shape to nebulous drift.

IV.

How experience fills up with words, becomes mute.
How memory is carried in a scent or a single note
of a single song. How what aches is also what saves.
How I feel like an island in a vast sea, sloshed over
by water, gasping, gasping and at low tide,
limning the invisible with my sighs.

V.

Crow rests on the back of my chair, sighs into my hair
as I sift the words in my cupped hands. Find just the one,
let it go.

First Snowfall

for Alex

I.

It is impossible to catch snow this wet
in your hands. It lasts only moments
even in the hair or on the branch.
I still hold out my palms like I can
catch it, like I can draw you right
out of my consciousness and back
into the crystalline shape of ice.

> *Just to put my hands on your ears,*
> *cradle your head with my love,*
> *this would be the right way*
> *to say goodbye.*

It was a hard year. We were tired
of farewells, I suppose. We had tasted
their permanence so immediately,
were aware of what re-emerges—
and what truly departs—
when the season changes.

II.

Your snowball packed my nose with ice.
I howled my sadness into your t-shirt that day,
you on your knees in the cold. So patient.
Quiet in our waning winter.
It had added itself up, that grief—during the days
I fed you chili and soup and everything
I knew that spoke love to the belly. Healing.
Your snow angel had left you, and the spring
was already pushing its way into our lives.
Then it was big and unwieldy and finally,
with the sanction of a snowball, it spilled itself,
left its mark: the shape of my face in mascara tears
on the front of your t-shirt.

"Is there black under my eyes?" I asked you.
"There's black on your chin," you said, grinning,
your Rhone-colored eyes apologetic for the clumsiness
of your comfort. Later, we would laugh about falling
to pieces. Laughter without mirth, but imbued
with our appreciation for the other. Appreciation
for how imperfect we are. How perfect.

> *Just turn your head and listen,*
> *I am there, I've always been.*
> *We crane our heads to know*
> *the invisible. We open our mouths*
> *to murmur the words...*

But that was ages ago. Or minutes.
The season is shifting again, how many
have there been? The air becomes cold,
trees prepare to carry the weight of winter
again. You are far away, and the mountain
still echoes that name.

Your statue stands near my window now, tongue
extended like mine, only he catches the white square
that will usher him into dreams more vivid than life—
so many ways to minister to the grieving.

I contemplate the difference between a snowflake
and that square, between your love and mine,
and know that goodbye is only a word,
spirit a promise that transcends taste buds
and the happy distortion of the melancholy.

Meditation on a Train from Rome

for Daryl

My eyes close as the train departs the Rome
terminal, and immediately I am tiptoeing
from star to star, waving my arms like thin flags,
gyrations of physical language, messages to the
next galaxy. *We are here, we are here, we are—*

After Florence, Alice looks at me and asks if
maybe I'm hiding. The question circles my ears
in its precarious orbit, carries the meaning I have
considered at intervals. I can nearly touch it
with my tongue as it comes 'round, birthed into
visibility, panting its comment on my life, this place,
each conversation I have. Each eye I catch and hold,
even for a moment.

I am hiding from all of this, how it rises in my gorge
like bile, like fear. One Italian woman, white haired
and round shouldered sits bundled and with a heavy
trunk at the station in Florence. I watch her as her
bench speeds away from me. So many people, so many
individual intentions, all crossing each other, obscuring one
another, colliding and tangling until it all feels like
static. Like a white noise that will not soothe
but grates against the eardrum, reminds us
of the futility of our acts. It slows and becomes
muffled, hisses into stillness, for an instant, each
time we stop. But never silence.

After Bologna I float up into the sky, trailing my shoes, my
clothes, this cumbersome thought-hat, into the space
of language. I shake memory from my hair, let it
sprinkle down, watch it ignite as it enters
the earth's atmosphere. Tiny comets of reminiscence
blazing in my peripheral vision. Then disappearing
without a sound.

Rising, I step gingerly onto the first star and begin
the navigation. The train is miles from me now,
just pulling into Milan. It is invisible. Traces of a
sound, of a thought—then gone with the other firey
fragments. I make my way across the black
vastness and concentrate on my own steady breath,
the other figures who move in my vicinity.
The way the stars light our bodies from underneath
our gossamer skirts, our cloaks of tulle. Everything
is new here. Clean. Spacious and real, imbued
with our senses, what it takes to wake them.

Here, we have no history and no future—Well—
there is a putti who carries them under his tongue,
just in case we remember about time, but he is busy
keeping Michelangelo company, one dose of water
from the River Lethe at a time.

Remembrance

He decides to write about Spencer,
the boy who disappeared into snow,
into my first cold winter here.
When it snows again this year, I am

distraught. I cry with French-speaking
strangers in the télécabine. They politely
turn away from me, the way all the people
on the plane to California did—

the day I cried and cried and tried
to climb into the Chiclet-shaped hollow
the double-paned window made
next to my head. It was impossible

to crawl away from them, I knew,
but it didn't stop me trying. My
chicken pasta curdled on my seat-back
tray as I hid, shuddering softly in my

invented privacy, and the girl next to me
let her hand fall onto my hip as she slept,
jaw wagging open, the gray wad of her gum
tucked between her tongue and her left molars.

That day I was crying for something else,
something I could not name but later
identified as having to do with my mom, who
wasn't facing chemotherapy or the indignity of

shitting into a bag attached to her stomach,
but who had stood with her hand on my dad's
heart a full year, denying even her most basic needs,
as he did these things in tears of his own.

In a way it was me, he writes, *who died
on the mountain that day,* and I marvel

at such frankness, the way he means
what he says and how he furrows his brow

in the effort of speaking truth. How we are so
fragile, so boisterous. How in spring it's hard
to remember the lines of the hills covered in snow.
How in winter it's hard to remember the grass.

Dear Bill Rasmovicz

It occurs to me that it is as likely
that nothing is sacred as that everything is

but standing on a corner in the Monasteraki,
mid-June in smelly Athens, a white-haired woman

in a polka-dotted dress shows me her teeth,
an immodest grin. She rides on a red moped,

her pomaded nephew wedged tightly between
her crinkly knees and reflecting the whole city

in his sunglasses. It is hard to get my head around
how convincing you are when you say, 'This is all

there is' and suggest that even this might secretly be
nothing. It occurs to me that we grow old. Our beauty

fades and hope is edged with something like coal. Like
kohl. I believe you when you speak of the 'myth

of ourselves' but when I lay it down next to the way a
Greek couple huddles together to keep their dog warm

on a ferry to Santorini, swaddle it in a t-shirt that says,
"I Love NY," I don't know if I can accept the unreality

of things as they are. There are just a few things
I believe in. A few things that whisk cynicism

from around my ears, disentagle it from my hair
and leave me crying.

El Retiro

Madrid, 2007

It's as if the sky will split open like the belly
of a fish, rain all of its iridescent scales down
on our heads, be the thing we seek no more.

It slips through hands in cold, clear water,
limbless muscle of our wanting. Liquid breath
finds its way through clenching of gills—

retracting like rib cages as we struggle to breathe
what forces its way into our hearts, cleaves us
open like skies like fish like mouths parting

with words that want to be spoken, want to stream
into the air—parade themselves while we shrink
from the truths they carry on their heads, linguistic

spines erect and, baskets overflowing with every
thing we cannot admit. How it aches how it aches
this prising of our hearts our teeth our bones. Oh.

It bursts into air, explodes hypocrisy, detonates
pretense and leaves us soft and panting, tongues
flaccid in our pulsing heads. We are seven hundred

Spaniards strolling in the Retiro, we are bronze lions
lifting faces toward the clock tower over the most
beautiful post office in the world. Trees stretch barren

limbs like fleshless hands into the sky, Spanish flag
waving just beyond in answer to their wordless question.
And the fountain in the plaza sings its liquid song, light

moving through its trajectory, all golden in its arcing
sigh. This is the way we remember, how we let the past
translate itself into any given moment, let the future lay

itself down on the bed of our hatreds and flex its heart, simultaneously the threat of coming into being and the promise to pull us into itself, make us moan.

Evolution

There was a time we were underwater, eyes
open wide. Bubbles clung to eyelashes,
hair fanned out like kelp. There was no sound
there, no vision but the deep—and light
in shifting beams, piercing the aqueous
canopy above. Skin was pale, textured with
cold—imagining the air, the unmitigated
sun, sand in hands, the blessing of breath.
Where are you? Voices carried the question
like beauty, like pain, spilled it over the lip
of higher consciousness.

> *Crows descend onto white branches*
> *punctuated with red berries.*
> *Lift off again, shaking snow from*
> *black and spindly feet.*

II.

And then…on land. There was so much hurt.
We struggled with what did not match the picture
that anyone else drew in the sand. We thought to
turn and give it away, rather than let it burn in our
hands, become the thing that we really desire.
Oh—pensive sound of dis-connection, how we
finally must somehow rise, burst into blackness,
take flight—no way of coming back, no way to
shed feathers that glisten with our perfect want.

> *Crows in flight, black feet tangled,*
> *beaks clacking softly, feathers slick*
> *and sliding off one another as they rise,*
> *given to abandon.*

IV.

And now, in the ether: sunshine and stars—
unexpected harmony, unsought fidelity, surprise of
like constitution. It is how we accept that some things
do not fit in our conception of the world. What I see
in your eyes rattles me, lifts me, inspirits me—is this mine?
Oh, god. I quake to think of it. But I embrace it just the same,
with the intrepidity of the faithful.

"To die without perishing is to be truly
present," sighs the Crow, and we,
we breathe it, too. Lift our crow heads
skyward, turn our crow backs to the
darkness of disbelief.

What We Agree To

for Gondry, Kaufman and Bismuth

Clouds slide across a slick sky,
harbingers of the regret that will be mine
in .2 seconds when the door clicks shut
behind me, and the moss begins to grow
and creep over the porous surface of my
stone resolve. *Daffodils have no scent,*
but they are so pretty, you said,
and I knew what was already past,
could taste the present on my tongue
like an acrid pill. *I won't stay,*
I said aloud in my head, but
I was the only one there—you could not
hear me in the recesses of my brain.

Atrophied heart twitches in the cave
of my chest, clove of disdain smokes itself
between my fingers. *I can see the future,*
I say, and you don't begin to discern
my anticipation of heat generated by discord,
only now emerging in my blood, seeing you
touch me as from far away—and through
liquid maybe. The way we suffer the cold
to create possibility, if only a small one.
Invite wind into a space and let it lift our hair,
knowing the price of abandon.
Okay, you say, and you show me
that you want everything in between.
That the leaving is insignificant.

Kim Cope Tait earned her MFA in Writing at Vermont College of Fine Arts in 2000. Her work has appeared in literary journals and magazines in the U.S. and abroad. She has two novels, *Inertia* and *Bend the Blue Sky*, as well as a chapbook of poems entitled *Element*. Kim also wrote and recorded *Lotus Wheel: Guided Meditations for Relaxation and Healing* in 2013. Having lived in Hawai'i, Switzerland, New Zealand, Vermont, and Colorado, Kim now lives with her family and teaches in her hometown of Santa Cruz, California.

www.ingramcontent.com/pod-product-compliance
Lightning Source LLC
Chambersburg PA
CBHW021202090426
42740CB00008B/1192